Animal Tales

Retold by **James Butler**
Activities by **Claudia Fiocco**

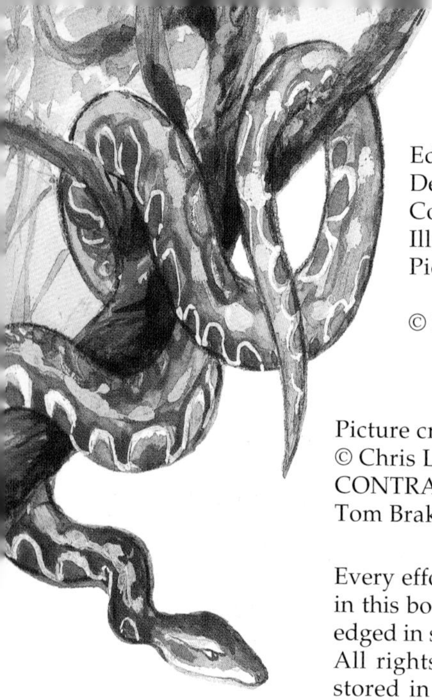

Editors: Emma Berridge, Frances Evans
Design and art direction: Nadia Maestri
Computer graphics: Simona Corniola
Illustrations: Eugene Collilieux, Franco Grazioli
Picture research: Laura Lagomarsino

Picture credits:
© Chris Lisle / CONTRASTO: 26-28; © Gallo Images / CONTRASTO: 27, 67; © Paul A. Souders / CONTRASTO: 29; © Tom Brakefield / CONTRASTO: 68-69.

We would be happy to receive your comments and suggestions, and give you any other information concerning our material.
editorial@blackcat-cideb.com
www.blackcat-cideb.com
www.cideb.it

CISQ CISQCERT
TEXTBOOKS AND TEACHING MATERIALS
The quality of the publisher's design, production and sales processes has been certified to the standard of
UNI EN ISO 9001

ISBN 88-530-0014-7 Book
ISBN 88-530-0015-5 Book + CD

Printed in Italy by Litoprint, Genoa

CONTENTS

Introduction 5

Notes on *the Authors* 6

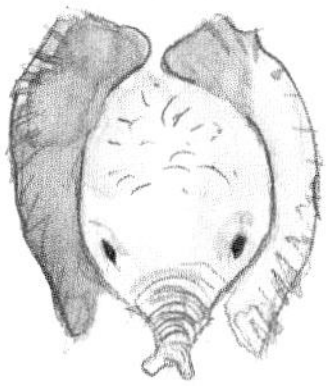

The Elephant's Child by Rudyard **Kipling**

PART **ONE** The Elephant's Child wants some answers 11

PART **TWO** The great, grey, green Limpopo River 15

PART **THREE** The Elephant's Child and the crocodile 20

Elephants 26

INTERNET PROJECT 30

Pigs is Pigs by Ellis **Parker Butler**

PART **ONE** The correct price for pigs 33

PART **TWO** Letters about pigs 38

PART **THREE** Pigs will never be pigs again 44

Mrs Packletide's Tiger by **Saki**

PART **ONE** Mrs Packletide shoots a tiger 56

PART **TWO** Triumph and disaster 62

Tigers *the world's largest cats* 67

INTERNET PROJECT 70

The Stolen White Elephant by Mark **Twain**

PART **ONE** A royal present 73

PART **TWO** Inspector Blunt gives his orders 80

PART **THREE** The end of the case 86

The Shameful Behaviour of a Fox Terrier

from *Three Men in a Boat* by Jerome K. **Jerome**

PART **ONE** The Haymarket Stores 97

PART **TWO** Montmorency 103

ACTIVITIES 5, 8, 14, 18, 24, 36, 42, 50, 60, 65, 77, 85, 91, 102, 106

EXIT TEST 107

TAPESCRIPTS 109

KEY TO THE **EXIT TEST** 112

PET Cambridge Preliminary English Test-style exercises

T: GRADE Trinity-style exercises (Grade 4)

This story is recorded in full.

END These symbols indicate the beginning and end of the extracts linked to the listening activities.

Introduction

In this collection of animal tales there are two main types of stories.

In 'The Elephant's Child' and 'The Shameful Behaviour of a Fox Terrier' the animals are without question the main characters, they are the so-called protagonists. The reader's attention is completely focused on them, their characteristics and their almost human behaviour. The animals speak amongst themselves, and all this seems quite normal to the reader.

The other type of stories includes 'Pigs is Pigs', 'Mrs Packletide's Tiger' and 'The Stolen White Elephant'. In these stories the animals are not the main characters. They behave like 'real' animals. The reader knows little about them and sometimes the animals are imaginary; we never really 'see' them. The authors' intent is not to write about the animals, but to ridicule [1] certain types of behaviour in our society.

Before you read these stories make a list of all the animals you know.

Then write down some words to describe them, for example:

Animal: cat/kitten: tail, whiskers, paws, soft etc.

While you read the following stories add any new words you learn to your list. It will be interesting to see how many new words connected to animals you include.

1. **ridicule** : laugh about.

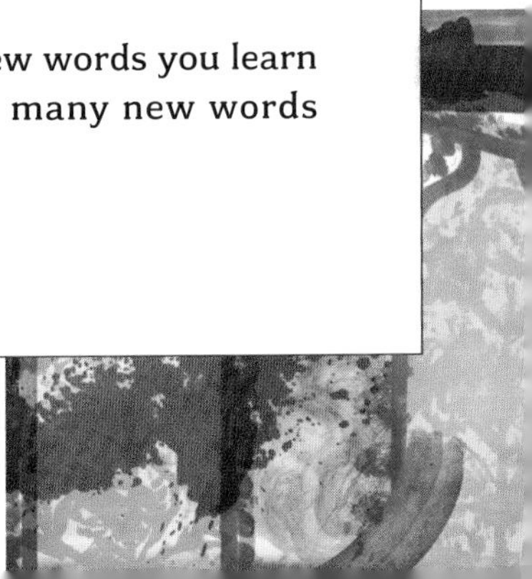

Notes on *the Authors*

'The Elephant's Child' by Rudyard Kipling (1865-1936) comes from his collection of *Just So Stories* (1902) which also contains stories about other types of animals. Kipling began to write these stories when he visited South Africa. That is probably why this story is not set in India where he was born.

'Pigs is Pigs' is by Ellis Parker Butler (1869-1937). He was born in Muscatine, Iowa, USA. He published 2,200 stories, books, essays and poems and is best known for the story in this collection of *Animal Tales*.

'Mrs Packletide's Tiger', set in India and England, is by Saki, Hector Hugh Munro (1870-1916). Saki was born in Burma, a now independent republic called Myanmar in south-east Asia, but returned to London because he could no longer serve in the Burma police.
In London he began to write political satires for *The Westminster Gazette.* He died while fighting during WWI.

Mark Twain, Samuel Langhorne Clemens (1835-1910), wrote 'The Stolen White Elephant', a hilarious [1] satire about the New York police. Although Mark Twain was a prolific writer he is probably best remembered as the American author of *The Adventures of Tom Sawyer* (1876).

'The Shameful Behaviour of a Fox Terrier' comes from *Three Men in a Boat* (1889) by Jerome K(lapka) Jerome (1859-1927). Jerome was born near Staffordshire and moved to East London where he became an actor and a reporter before becoming a writer. Although the story is actually about a boating holiday on the River Thames, the extract included here is indeed about a fox terrier.

Other Black Cat Reading and Training titles by some of these same authors include:
The Jumping Frog by Mark Twain – beginner
The £1,000,000 Bank Note by Mark Twain – elementary
Three Men and a Boat by Jerome K. Jerome – elementary
Wicked and Humorous Tales by Saki – pre-intermediate

1. **hilarious** : very funny.

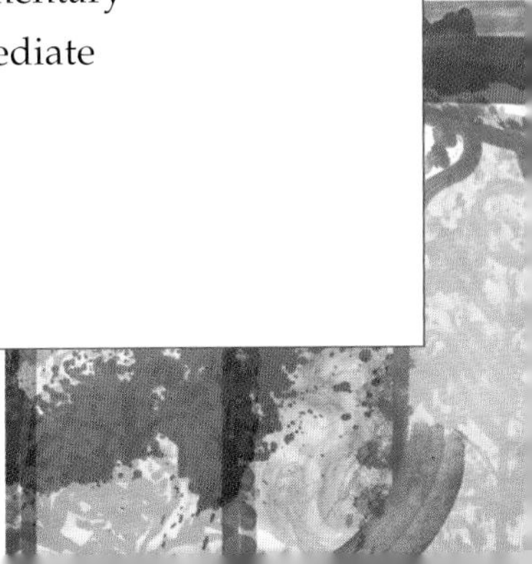

INTERNET PROJECT

Divide the class into 5 groups. Each group must find out 5 things about the authors of this collection of *Animal Tales*. If you have access to a computer your teacher will be able to give you some useful web addresses.

When you have collected all the material, first check to see that it is reliable, then report your findings to the rest of the class.

Write your 5 things here:

1. ....
2. ....
3. ....
4. ....
5. ....

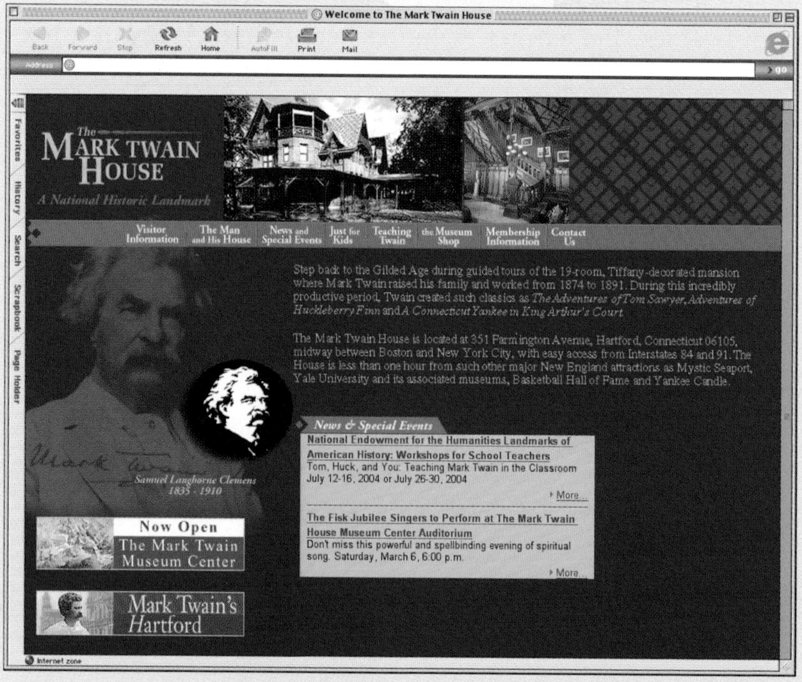

The Elephant's Child

by Rudyard **Kipling**

Before you read

1 Look at the animals shown in the pictures on pages 13 and 17 and list them in the table below (if you are not sure guess or compare your opinions with another student). Use a dictionary or an encyclopedia to list the main characteristics of each species.

	Animal	Characteristics
Reptiles		*air-breathing vertebrates* *they are cold-blooded*
Birds		
Mammals		

2 Use a dictionary or an encyclopedia to list the main characteristics of herbivores and carnivores, then say if the animals you listed above are herbivores or carnivores.

3 Look at the words (1-3) below and match them to the appropriate country (a-c).

1. ☐ jungle/forest
2. ☐ wood
3. ☐ bush

a. Australia
b. Africa
c. England

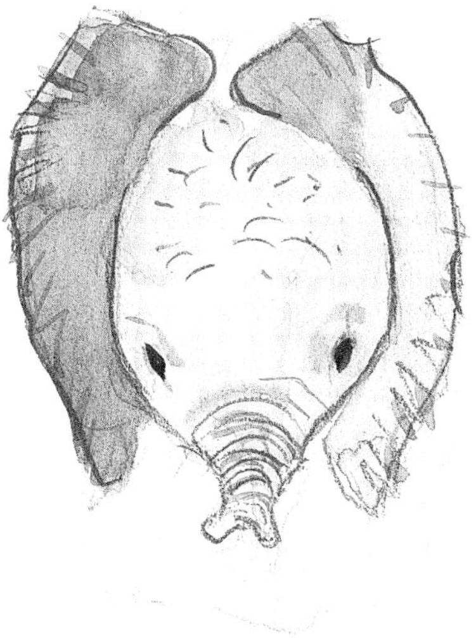

PART ONE

The Elephant's Child wants some answers

In the beginning elephants had noses. They had large noses, but they could not pick things up [1] with them.

One day the Elephant's Child began to ask everybody questions. He always asked a lot of questions. He asked his aunt the ostrich:

'Why have you got long feathers?' [2]

1. **pick things up** : lift/hold things up.

2. **feathers** : 

The ostrich was angry with the Elephant's Child. She punished him [1] and sent him away.

'Don't ask questions, Elephant's Child!' she told him.

The Elephant's Child then went to his uncle the giraffe.

'Why have you got spots?' [2] he asked the giraffe.

His uncle the giraffe was angry with the Elephant's Child. He punished him and sent him away.

'Don't ask questions, Elephant's Child!' he told him.

The Elephant's Child now went to his aunt the hippopotamus.

'Why have you got red eyes?' he asked his aunt.

The hippopotamus was angry, and she, too, punished the Elephant's Child.

'Don't ask questions!' she told him.

The Elephant's Child now went to his uncle the baboon.

'Why do you like melons?' he asked. 'Why are they good to eat?'

The baboon was angry and he punished the Elephant's Child.

'Don't ask questions, Elephant's Child!' he told him.

One day the Elephant's Child had a new question.

'What does the crocodile eat?' he asked everybody.

'Be quiet, Elephant's Child!' everybody shouted at him.

His uncles and aunts were angry with the Elephant's Child. They all punished him for a long time. He was very unhappy. He went away for a walk in the forest.

1. **punished him** : (here) hit him because he did something wrong.

2. **spots** : 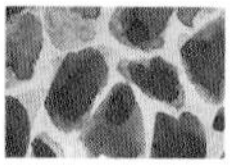

Go back to the text

PET **1** **Based on what you read in this part of the story and your general knowledge, decide if each statement is correct or incorrect. If it is correct, write A. If it is incorrect, write B.**

1 The Elephant's Child lived in Africa.
2 Elephants did not have noses in the beginning.
3 Ostriches only live in Africa.
4 The Elephant's Child didn't ask many questions.
5 The animals punished the Elephant's Child.
6 The Elephant's Child's uncles were the giraffe and the baboon.
7 Hippopotamuses have red eyes.
8 The Latin name for melons is *cucumis melo*.
9 This was the Elephant's Child question: 'What does the crocodile eat?'
10 His aunts and uncles were happy with the Elephant's Child.

1	2	3	4	5 .....
6	7	8	9	10 .....

Now correct the incorrect statements.

T: GRADE 4

2 **Topic – Animals and Pets**
Tell the class about your favourite animal or pet. Bring a picture of the animal or pet to class and use these questions/statements to help you.

a. What is your favourite animal or pet?
b. Compare your pet to an animal that lives in the wild.
c. When did you get your pet?
d. Describe the things your pet or animal does and the ways it does them.

Now think of a question to ask the students in the class about their favourite animal or pet.

PART TWO

The Great, Grey, Green Limpopo River

The Elephant's Child met the Kolokolo bird [1] in the forest. He told the Kolokolo bird everything.

'My father punished me, my uncles punished me, and my aunts punished me,' he said. 'What does the crocodile eat? Do you know?'

The Kolokolo bird thought for a moment, then he said.

'Do you know the great, grey, green Limpopo River?'

'Yes,' replied the Elephant's Child. 'I know it.'

1. **Kolokolo bird** : an imaginary bird.

'Go there,' the Kolokolo bird told the Elephant's Child. 'You can ask there.'

'I'll go there immediately!' the Elephant's Child decided.

The Elephant's Child walked through the forest until he came to the great, grey, green Limpopo River. Then he saw a python snake.

'Excuse me,' he said, 'but is there a crocodile here?'

'Yes,' the python snake told him. 'A crocodile lives here.'

'Good,' replied the Elephant's Child. 'What does he eat?'

The python was angry now, and he punished the Elephant's Child.

'Don't ask questions, Elephant's Child!' he told him.

The Elephant's Child walked some more. He walked on something big. It was the crocodile!

The Elephant's Child looked down.

'Where is the crocodile?' he asked politely.

The crocodile opened one eye very slowly. He looked at the Elephant's Child.

'Come here, Elephant's Child,' he said quietly. 'I'm the crocodile.'

'Good!' cried the Elephant's Child. 'What do you eat?'

'Come here,' the crocodile told him again.

The Elephant's Child came very close to the crocodile. The crocodile opened his mouth very wide. He held the Elephant's Child by the nose.

'Today,' said the crocodile, 'I think I'll eat an Elephant's Child!'

Go back to the text

PET **1** **For each question, tick (✓) the letter next to the correct answer, A, B, C or D.**

1 What does the reader learn about the great, grey, green Limpopo River?

A ☐ It is a very big, grey, green river in an African forest.
B ☐ Pythons live in the river.
C ☐ It is the longest river in Africa.
D ☐ The river is always grey and green.

2 How does the Elephant's Child ask the question 'Where is the crocodile?'?

A ☐ Rudely.
B ☐ Politely.
C ☐ Quickly.
D ☐ Slowly.

3 Why did the Elephant's Child walk on the crocodile?

A ☐ Because he didn't see the crocodile.
B ☐ Because he thought the crocodile was a bridge.
C ☐ Because the crocodile looked like a piece of wood.
D ☐ Because he wanted to make the crocodile angry.

4 What do you learn about what the crocodile eats?

A ☐ It usually eats insects and plants.
B ☐ It sometimes eats python snakes.
C ☐ It never eats animals.
D ☐ Today, it will eat the Elephant's Child.

5 Which Greek author do you think wrote fables about animals?

A ☐ Aesop.
B ☐ Dante.
C ☐ Shakespeare.
D ☐ Aristotle.

The great, grey, green Limpopo River

Order of adjectives

In English most adjectives go before the noun:
*The **great, grey, green** Limpopo River*

In this sentence the order of the adjectives is:

Size	Colour	Colour	Noun
(The) great	*grey*	*green*	*Limpopo River*

But be careful, adjectives usually go after the following verbs:
be, seem, look, become: *The python was **angry.***

2 **Make a list of adjectives that describe feelings (for example, angry, happy, annoyed, curious) and write five sentences about the different animals in the story.**

Here is an example: *The Elephant's Child was curious.*

a. ....

b. ....

c. ....

d. ....

e. ....

3 **Look at the order of adjectives above and write complete sentences about each animal. (Use a dictionary to look up the words you don't know).**

Example: Elephants (mammals/grey/brown/large)
Elephants are large, grey, brown mammals.

a. Pythons (multi-coloured/carnivores/long)
b. Ostriches (long-necked/birds/brown/black)
c. Crocodiles (reptiles/long-snouted/green/brown)
d. Eagles (birds of prey/large/black and white)
e. Hippopotamuses (grey/brown/large/amphibious mammals)

PART THREE

The Elephant's Child and the crocodile

The python snake arrived at that moment.

He said to the Elephant's Child, 'The crocodile will eat you, my friend. You must pull as hard as you can. Pull, my young friend, pull!'

The Elephant's Child pulled and he pulled. It was no good.[1] His nose was still in the crocodile's mouth.

The crocodile also pulled as hard as he could. He pulled and he pulled.

1. **it was no good** : (here) the problem was not solved.

E.G.

The Elephant's Child's nose began to grow longer and longer. Suddenly the Elephant's Child gave an extra hard pull — and he was free! He sat back on the ground. His nose was very long now, and very warm. He put it into the great, grey, green Limpopo River for a moment.

'Why are you doing that?' asked the python snake.

'My nose is too long,' the Elephant's Child told him. 'Perhaps the river will make it small again.'

'Your nose will always be like that now,' the python told him.

'But I don't like it!' cried the Elephant's Child.

'Perhaps you'll like it one day,' the python said. 'But it isn't a nose any more. It's too long for a nose. We'll call it a trunk.' [1]

The Elephant's Child was not very happy at all. At that moment a mosquito flew [2] onto the Elephant's Child's head. The Elephant's Child lifted his trunk and hit the mosquito. The mosquito flew away.

'A trunk is a good thing!' the python said. 'It's very useful.'

The Elephant's Child began to play with his new trunk. He picked up some grass. He ate the grass happily.

'Now tell me something,' said the python. 'Do people hit and punish you? Do you like that?'

'Of course not!' replied the Elephant's Child. 'I don't like it at all.'

The python smiled at him.

1. **trunk** : 

2. **flew** : past of 'to fly'.

'Now you've got a trunk,' he said. 'Now you can hit and punish them!'

The Elephant's Child smiled too.

'That's an idea,' he said slowly. 'A very good idea!'

He walked home. When he arrived, all his uncles and aunts were happy to see him.

'Come here, Elephant's Child!' they cried.

The Elephant's Child moved towards them. He smiled happily.

One by one he punished his uncles and his aunts with his new trunk.

'Where did you get the new nose?' they asked him.

'It's not a nose,' the Elephant's Child told them. 'It's a trunk. I asked the crocodile what he eats. Then he gave me the trunk.'

'We want trunks, too!' all the elephants cried. They ran off to the great, grey, green Limpopo River. When they found the crocodile, they asked him:

'What do you eat?'

The crocodile pulled their noses. And now all elephants have got trunks.

Go back to the text

PET **1** **Based on what you read in the story and your general knowledge, decide if each statement is correct or incorrect. If it is correct, write A. If it is incorrect, write B.**

1 The python snake told the Elephant's Child to push.
2 The crocodile ate the Elephant's Child.
3 The Elephant's Child's nose was now small and sore.
4 The python called the Elephant's Child's nose a trunk.
5 The Elephant's Child hit the mosquito with its ear.
6 The Elephant's Child discovered that trunks are very useful.
7 He punished his uncles and aunts.
8 The Elephant's Child did not tell them the story about his trunk.
9 The other elephants wanted trunks, too.
10 Not all elephants have trunks today.

1	2	3	4	5 .....
6	7	8	9	10 .....

Now correct the incorrect statements.

2 **Find the following expressions in the chapter and use them to complete the sentences on page 25.**

a. longer (and) longer
b. (an extra hard) pull
c. perhaps (you'll) like
d. hit
e. useful

1. 'Is it .... to learn English pronunciation?' 'Yes, it is. Actually, it depends.'
2. 'Does *eat* rhyme with .... ?' 'No, it doesn't.'
3. 'Does an extra hard .... mean it's very strong medicine?' 'No, of course it doesn't. What you are thinking of is, "a very strong (headache) pill." Pill rhymes with *ill* (sick). .... rhymes with bull.'
4. 'I am spending .... and .... learning English. I don't like it any more.'
5. '................................ you'll .... it again one day. Just remember to do your homework every day.'

3 **A fable is a short, funny story, usually with animals as characters, which tells us a moral. Think about 'The Elephant's Child'. Find three similar fables from your country. Write their titles and list their characteristics.**

1. **Title:** ....
   Characteristic: ....
   ....
2. **Title:** ....
   Characteristic: ....
   ....
3. **Title:** ....
   Characteristic: ....
   ....

Elephants

There are two main types of elephants. The photo you see on this page represents *Elephas maximus*. It lives in Asia and has small ears. Only the male of the species has long incisor teeth called tusks.

Indian elephant walking through Periyar Reserve in India.

Loxodonta africana, as the name suggests, comes from Africa and has very large ears. Both males and females usually have tusks. Even though there are some differences between these two main species, they have a lot in common. Study this list of common features of elephants.

- The ancestors of elephants first appeared 45-55 million years ago
- These ancestors were less than 1 metre tall and had no trunk
- Elephants live in groups, called herds
- Mature females (matriarchs) lead the herds
- Baby elephants are called calves
- Females have calves until they are fifty years old

African elephant family group.

- Lions, leopards and tigers hunt and kill calves
- Elephants have poor eyesight
- Their trunks help them to eat, drink, wash, feel where they are going and socialise
- Elephants can hold up to four litres of water in their trunk

Working elephant lifting logs.
In the past, people used elephants to move heavy logs. This is less common today as people are interested in conserving the species.

‘Elephants never forget’

There is a common saying ‘Elephants never forget’. There is now scientific proof that this saying is correct. The scientific study revealed that females leading the group build a social memory. This enables them to recognise ‘friendly faces’ and protect the rest of the herd.

The older the dominant matriarch becomes the more memory she has. The group feels safe. The safer they feel the more time they can spend relaxing and breeding.[1]

When people kill elephants for their ivory tusks they often kill the oldest members of the group. This makes it very difficult for the group to survive. Killing elephants also affects the environment, because these animals help keep ecosystems stable.

Bull elephant by setting sunlight.

1. **breeding** : having calves.

INTERNET PROJECT

Your teacher will give you a list of web addresses where you can find out more information about these magnificent animals.

Try and find out about:

- what the male elephant's role is
- how long an elephant lives on average
- why elephants are in danger
- how people are helping them
- in which cultures elephants are important and why
- which schools are involved in a 'save the elephant' programme
- more common features to add to the list on page 28

Once you have finished your research share your findings with the rest of the class. You can always organise a 'trivial pursuit' type game with the information you have collected.

Pigs is Pigs

by Ellis **Parker Butler**

Before you read

1 Look at the pictures on pages 35, 40 and 49. Where and when do you think the story takes place?

2 Focus on the people you see in the pictures. What are the people wearing? What do they look like?

3 What do you think will happen in the story?

4 Which of the animals below are usually considered domestic pets?

a. ☐ cats	d. ☐ canaries	g. ☐ tigers
b. ☐ dogs	e. ☐ snakes	h. ☐ goldfish
c. ☐ pigs	f. ☐ sheep	i. ☐ eagles

5 Make the plural words above singular.

6 Use a dictionary to help you match the expressions below (1-4) to their meanings (a-d).

1. ☐ to pig out
2. ☐ to be pig-headed
3. ☐ a piggy bank
4. ☐ a pigtail

a. to be very obstinate in a stupid way
b. to eat and behave like a pig
c. a plait of hair (many native American women wore plaits)
d. a money box usually kept by children in the shape of a pig

PART ONE

The correct price for pigs

Mr Flannery worked for the Interurban Express Company. The company delivered parcels all over America. This morning Mr Flannery was very angry. His customer, Mr Morehouse, was also very angry.

'You decide!' shouted Mr Flannery.

He indicated the box in front of him. The box contained two small guinea pigs.[1] They were happy to eat their food.

'You can pay for them and take them away. Or you can leave them here. But rules[2] are rules, Mr Morehouse!'

'You're an idiot!' shouted Mr Morehouse. 'The company rules are very clear — look!'

Mr Morehouse indicated a book on the counter. Then he read aloud.

1. **guinea pigs** : 

2. **rules** : regulations.

'Domestic pets in boxes, Franklin to Westcote, 25 cents each.'

'These are domestic pets, they're in boxes, and they came from Franklin to Westcote. I'll pay 25 cents each. There are two of them. I'll pay you 50 cents!'

Mr Flannery picked up the rulebook. Now he began to read what it said.

'I know they're domestic pets,' Mr Flannery said angrily. 'And the price for domestic pets is 25 cents. But they're also pigs; I know that, too. And the price for pigs is 30 cents each. You'll have to pay 30 cents each — that's 60 cents for two.'

'That's ridiculous!' replied Mr Morehouse. 'That rule means ordinary pigs, not guinea pigs. It's obvious. The correct rate is 25 cents each.'

Mr Flannery was very stubborn. [1]

'Pigs are pigs,' he said. 'The company doesn't care. They are all pigs. Pigs are NOT domestic animals, and you must pay the rate [2] for pigs.'

Mr Morehouse was silent for a moment.

'Very well,' he said at last. 'I offered you 50 cents and you refused. I'll write to the President of the company and tell him everything. Keep the pigs. But you must look after them very well. Nothing must happen to them!'

Mr Morehouse left the office. Mr Flannery opened the box with the guinea pigs inside. He looked at them. They were happy. Mr Flannery was happy. He knew the rules about pigs.

1. **stubborn** : determined to do what he wants.
2. **rate** : price, cost.

E.C.

Go back to the text

PET **1** **Look at the six sentences for this part. Listen to Part One 'The Correct Price for Pigs'. Decide if each sentence is correct or incorrect. If it is correct, put a tick (✓) in the box under A for YES. If it is not correct, put a tick (✓) in the box under B for NO.**

5

		A YES	B NO
1	The Interurban Express Company was a type of postal service.	☐	☐
2	Mr Flannery was the customer and Mr Morehouse worked for the company.	☐	☐
3	The pigs in the box were guinea pigs.	☐	☐
4	The rate for domestic animals was 30 cents each.	☐	☐
5	Mr Morehouse offered 15 cents for the pigs.	☐	☐
6	Mr Flannery did not know the rules about pigs.	☐	☐

Prefixes

Here are some prefixes that are used to give the opposite meaning to words:

in — **in**correct = wrong

un — **un**happy = sad

2 **Use a dictionary to help you find the right prefix for the following words, then use them in sentences of your own.**

a. intelligent ....

b. able ....

c. experienced ....

d. effective ....

e. readable ....

'You must pay the rate for pigs'

Must/have to

The modal verb ***must*** is usually used to oblige us or someone else to do something.

Look at this example:
*School rules: You **must** wear a uniform.*

When we want to express a similar meaning in the future or in the past we use ***have to***.

Look at these examples:
*When you go to school you **will have to** wear a school uniform.* (future)
*When I went to school I **had to** wear a uniform.* (past)

3 **Complete the sentences below using the correct form of *must* or *have to*.**

- **a.** You .... pay the phone bill tomorrow.
- **b.** He is a good student, but he .... learn to be quiet in class.
- **c.** Everyone .... be here on time.
- **d.** A hundred years ago all farmers .... milk their cows by hand.
- **e.** When you visit the animal parks in South Africa, you .... follow the park rules.
- **f.** In the past, people .... kill animals to survive.
- **g.** You .... remember to do your homework every evening.

PART **TWO**

Letters about pigs

Mr Morehouse was very angry when he arrived home. He wrote a long letter to the President of the company. He explained the problem about the rate for the guinea pigs.

About a week later Mr Morehouse received a letter from the Interurban Express Company.

> Interurban Express Company
>
> Dear Sir,
>
> Please write to the claims department. [1]
>
> Yours faithfully [2]

1. **claims department** : part of a company which people contact when they are unhappy about something.
2. **yours faithfully** : formal way of ending a letter.

Mr Morehouse now wrote to the claims department of the company.

A few weeks later he received a reply from the claims department of the Interurban Express Company.

> Interurban Express Company
> Dear Sir,
> The pigs are in Mr Flannery's office. You did not pay anything to the company. You must write to the tariff department [1] about the correct rate for the delivery of the pigs.
> Yours faithfully

Mr Morehouse now wrote to the tariff department of the Interurban Express Company.

The manager of the tariff department, Mr Morgan, told his secretary to write to Mr Flannery.

'He didn't pay the domestic rate. Ask him to explain,' he ordered. 'And find out the present condition of the animals.'

Mr Flannery received the letter from the tariff department.

'Present condition of the animals,' he read. 'What does that mean? I'll look at them.'

He walked to the back of the office. There was a cage there. Mr Flannery looked inside. He began to count carefully.

1. **tariff department** : part of a company which decides the prices.

'One — two — three — four — five — six — seven — eight!' he counted. 'And all of them very well.'

Mr Flannery went back into his office and wrote to the tariff department of the company.

Dear Sir,
Pigs are pigs.
There are now eight pigs. They are all well.
They eat a lot. I paid $2.00 for their food.
Will Mr Morehouse pay for their food?
Yours faithfully

Mr Morgan, the head of the tariff department, read Mr Flannery's letter. He was very serious.

'Flannery is right!' he told his secretary. 'Pigs are pigs'. Then he wrote another letter to Mr Flannery.

Interurban Express Company
Dear Mr Flannery,
The rules are clear. When the animals
eat food the customer must pay for it.
Collect the $2.00 from Mr Morehouse.
Yours sincerely, [1]
Morgan

'Collect it!' Mr Flannery thought. 'I don't know how to do that.'

Suddenly he had an idea.

1. **yours sincerely** : a less formal way of ending a letter than 'yours faithfully'.

Go back to the text

PET **1** **Read the text below and choose the correct word for each space, mark the letter A, B, C, or D. There is an example at the beginning (0).**

Firstly, Mr Morehouse (**0**) ..A..... to the President (**1**) .... the company. He told Mr Morehouse to write to the claims (**2**) .... of the company. Mr Morehouse wrote to the claims department, (**3**) .... the claims department (**4**) .... him to write to the tariff department.

The tariff department wrote to Mr Flannery and asked (**5**) .... the present condition (**6**) .... the pigs. Mr Flannery replied, 'they are (**7**) .... They eat a lot. I spent $2.00 for (**8**) .... food. Who (**9**) .... pay for their food?'

Mr Morgan, the head of the tariff department, told Mr Flannery to (**10**) .... the money from the customer, Mr Morehouse.

0	**A** wrote	**B** said	**C** spoke	**D** told
1	**A** in	**B** at	**C** of	**D** for
2	**A** company	**B** warehouse	**C** office	**D** department
3	**A** when	**B** but	**C** so	**D** that
4	**A** told	**B** said	**C** shouted	**D** made
5	**A** on	**B** over	**C** about	**D** in
6	**A** of	**B** at	**C** in	**D** for
7	**A** well	**B** good	**C** better	**D** ill
8	**A** his	**B** their	**C** her	**D** its
9	**A** has	**B** had to	**C** must	**D** mustn't
10	**A** send	**B** bring	**C** give	**D** collect

2 Letters

At the beginning of Part Two Mr Morehouse wrote a long letter of complaint to the President of the company. Look at the copy of his letter below. You must complete it by deciphering the code. Be careful! The words are mixed up.

Dear Sir,

I am ●✥✥✹✱◆☆ a letter to ■☆♥✳❊✦❂✥ about the exact price I must pay to ♥✦●♥❂✦❖ my guinea pigs. The correct ✳◆❖● for guinea pigs is 25 cents. ✫❂✹◆✚❖❖, Mr Flannery, at your office, ✶✥✥✶☆✶● that I must pay 30 cents. He ✳✦✥♥✶■ that pigs are not domestic pets, but that they are pigs. This is ✖❂♣✥✥✖✦◆♥✶. I am ◆✳♣◆❖❊❖❊ to pay the correct price and no ❖❂■◆. If you do not ❊♥❖✳●♥ my offer I will ask my ✹✧✦❖✳◆ to write to you ✧❖♣❖✥✥✳●✦■■.

Yours ✧✦❄✖✫●❄✥✳✦,

Code:

a	b	c	d	e	f	g	h	i	l	m	n
✳	▲	♥	♣	❖	❄	✱	✫	✥	✦	■	☆

o	p	r	s	t	u	v	w	x	y	z
❂	❊	◆	✶	●	✖	✚	✹	❦	✧	✿

PART **THREE**

Pigs will never be pigs again

Mr Flannery drove to Mr Morehouse's house. Mr Morehouse smiled when he came out of the house.

'So you've brought the guinea pigs at last?' he said.

'No, sir,' replied Mr Flannery. 'I've got a bill for $2.00 for their food. Will you pay it?'

'$2.00!' exclaimed Mr Morehouse. 'For food for two guinea pigs. That's ridiculous! I certainly won't pay it.'

'There aren't two pigs,' Mr Flannery told him. 'There are eight of them now.'

Mr Morehouse closed the door of the house loudly. Mr Flannery drove back to his office.

Mr Flannery wrote again to Mr Morgan, the head of the tariff department. This time Mr Morgan spoke to the President of the Interurban Express Company.

'Are they domestic pets, or are they pigs?' Mr Morgan wanted to know.

The President thought for a moment, then he said,

'I don't know. I'll write to Professor Gordon. He's an expert. He'll know.'

Unfortunately, Professor Gordon was in South America. The letter from the President of the Interurban Express Company arrived after many months.

The President forgot about the problem, Mr Morgan forgot about the problem. Even Mr Morehouse forgot about the problem. Mr Flannery, however, did not forget about the problem. He wrote again to Mr Morgan.

Dear Mr Morgan,
What about these pigs? There are now
32 of them. They still eat a lot.
My office is now like a zoo! Shall I sell
the pigs?
Yours sincerely,
Flannery

Mr Morgan wrote back immediately.

Dear Mr Flannery,
Do not sell the pigs. They belong to Mr Morehouse. The company must continue to look after them.
Yours sincerely,
Morgan

Mr Flannery built a special place for the guinea pigs outside the office. A few months later he wrote to Mr Morgan again. His letter was very short.

Dear Mr Morgan,
160 pigs
Yours sincerely,
Flannery

At last a letter came from Professor Gordon. He explained everything to the President of the company. Guinea pigs are not pigs. They belong to a completely different family and species.

'Then the 25 cent rate is the correct one,' the President of the company decided. Mr Morgan now wrote to Mr Flannery.

Dear Mr Flannery,
Please deliver the 160 guinea pigs to Mr Morehouse. He must pay 25 cents for each guinea pig.
Yours sincerely,
Morgan

Mr Flannery wrote back immediately to Mr Morgan.

Dear Mr Morgan,
There are not 160 pigs. There are now 800. Do I have to charge [1] Mr Morehouse for 160 or for 800?
Yours sincerely,
Flannery

The Interurban Express Company considered the problem very carefully. This took time, and the number of guinea pigs increased every day. Now Mr Flannery counted 4,064 of them.

At last Mr Flannery received a letter from the company.

Interurban Express Company
Dear Mr Flannery,
Collect for two guinea pigs – 50 cents.
Deliver them all to Mr Morehouse.
Yours sincerely,
Morgan

Once again Mr Flannery drove to Mr Morehouse's home. Mr Morehouse did not live there any more. Mr Flannery asked the company for orders.

The company told him to send the guinea pigs to the head office of the Interurban Express Company.

1. **charge** : ask someone for an amount of money.

Mr Flannery began to send the cages of guinea pigs to the company. The company received cages of guinea pigs for days and days. Mr Flannery sent 280 cages in one week. The company now sent him a telegram.

> Interurban Express Company
> Stop sending guinea pigs.
> Warehouse [1] full

And Mr Flannery sent another telegram back.

> Can't stop. Flannery

The company sent an inspector to Mr Flannery's office. The company's wagon [2] was full of guinea pigs.

'That's the last of them!' shouted Mr Flannery angrily. 'I'll know what to do with animals next time,' he said. 'Forget the rules, that's what I'll do. Pigs are pets — cows are pets — horses are pets — and lions and tigers are pets. Everything goes at 25 cents!'

The wagon drove way with the last guinea pigs.

'There's one good thing,' Mr Flannery said happily. 'At least those pigs weren't elephants!'

1. **warehouse** : large building used to keep things in.
2. **wagon** : vehicle used to transport things.

Go back to the text

1 **Answer the questions below, put a tick (✓) in the box a or b, then turn to page 112 and add up your score. Your score must total 15. Play the game again until you score 15.**

1. In Part Three, Mr Flannery brought Mr Morehouse
   - a. ☐ the guinea pigs.
   - b. ☐ the bill.
2. What was the correct price for domestic animals?
   - a. ☐ 25 cents each.
   - b. ☐ 30 cents each.
3. The bill was for
   - a. ☐ the guinea pigs' food.
   - b. ☐ receiving the guinea pigs.
4. Professor Gordon said that guinea pigs were
   - a. ☐ not pigs.
   - b. ☐ of the same species as pigs.
5. Did Mr Morehouse pay for the guinea pigs' food?
   - a. ☐ Yes.
   - b. ☐ No.
6. Mr Morgan orders Mr Flannery to
   - a. ☐ deliver the 160 guinea pigs to Mr Morehouse.
   - b. ☐ charge Mr Morehouse 30 cents for each guinea pig.
7. The reply to Mr Flannery's question came
   - a. ☐ quickly.
   - b. ☐ slowly.
8. In the end
   - a. ☐ Mr Morehouse paid 50 cents for two guinea pigs.
   - b. ☐ Mr Flannery sent the now 4,064 guinea pigs to head office.

'So, you brought the guinea pigs at last,' Mr Morehouse said

Bring and **take**

We use ***bring*** when we want to suggest movement towards the speaker. ***Take*** is usually used for movement in other directions.

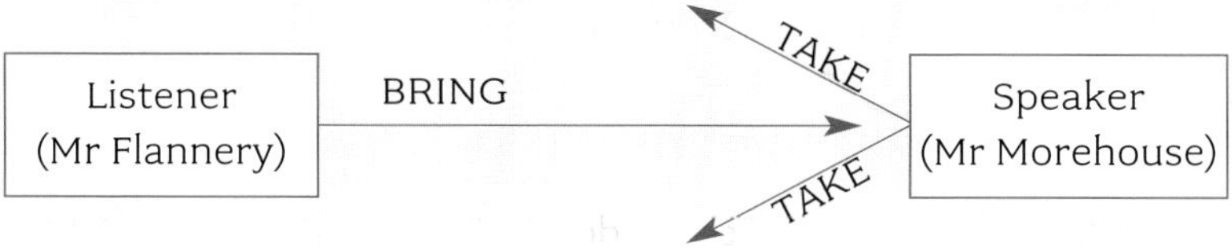

Look at these examples:

Mr Morehouse: *Come here and* ***bring*** *me my guinea pigs.*

Mr Flannery: *No, I will* ***take*** *them away with me.*

2 **Complete the dialogue below using either *bring* or *take* in the correct tense.**

a. 'John, please .... me my glasses'.
'Here you are, Mum.'

b. 'John, did you .... the dog out this morning?'

c. 'Yes, I .... it out before lunch.'

d. 'But the rubbish is still here, John. When are you going to .... it away?'

e. 'Okay, Mum. I'll .... you a nice cup of tea and then .... it out.'

f. 'Oh John, would you .... me some biscuits with my tea.'

g. 'Alright, Mum.'

h. 'And when you go out with the rubbish don't forget to .... the clothes to the laundry. And while you're at it, remember to .... those films to be developed. John are you listening? John? John? Are you listening to me?

Now listen to the recording to check your answers.

3 Practising numbers

1. Think of a number between 2-9.
2. Multiply it by 9.
3. Add the two digits together.
4. Subtract 5.
5. Think of that number as a letter of the alphabet.
6. Think of a European country beginning with that letter.
7. Think of an animal beginning with the second letter of that country.
8. Think of a typical colour for that animal.

Now turn to page 112.

4 Say if you agree or disagree with the following statements and then discuss them with your partner.

a. The title 'Pigs is Pigs' is grammatically incorrect. Why?

....

....

b. The title 'Pigs is Pigs' is about the meaning of pigs, i.e. the meaning of pigs is pigs.

....

....

c. To be fair and just, bureaucracy must always be rigid and inflexible.

....

....

d. It is easy to make clear rules.

....

....

Mrs Packletide's Tiger

by **Saki**

Before you read

PET 1 Listen to the first part of the story. For each question there are three pictures. Choose the correct picture and put a tick (✓) in the box below it.

1 What did Loona Bimberton do?

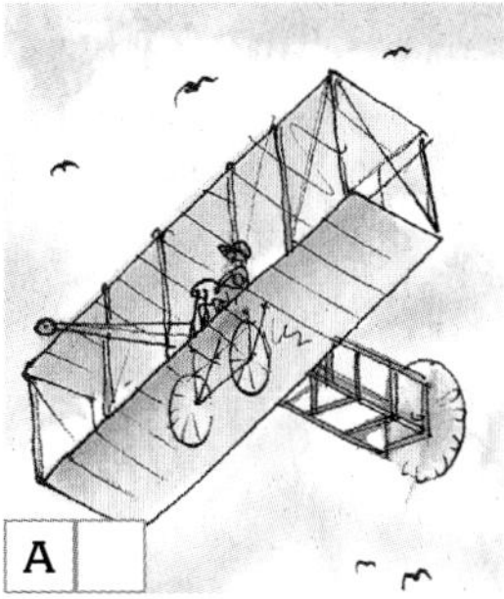

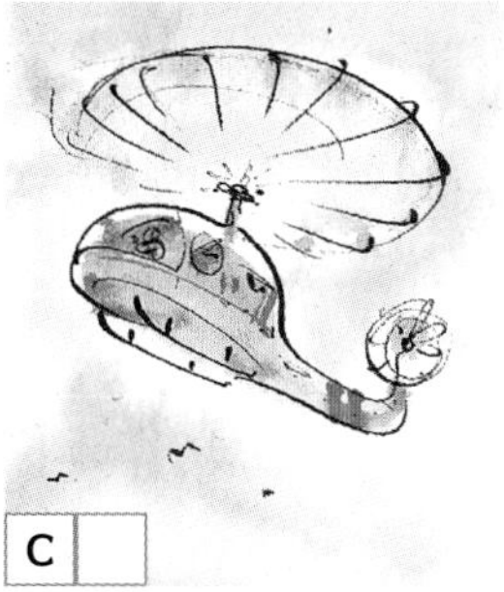

2 How much money did Mrs Packletide offer the Indians?

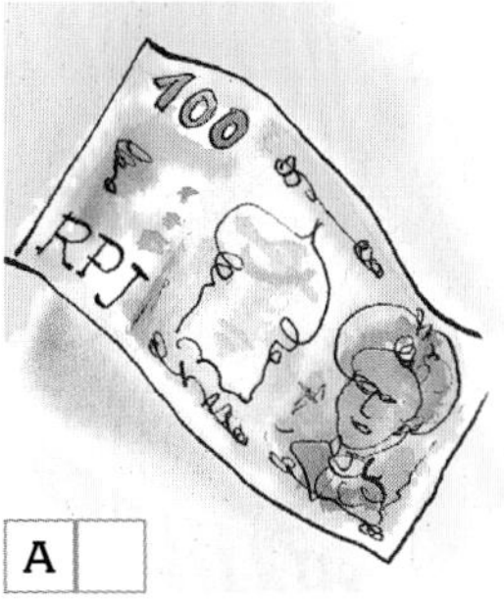

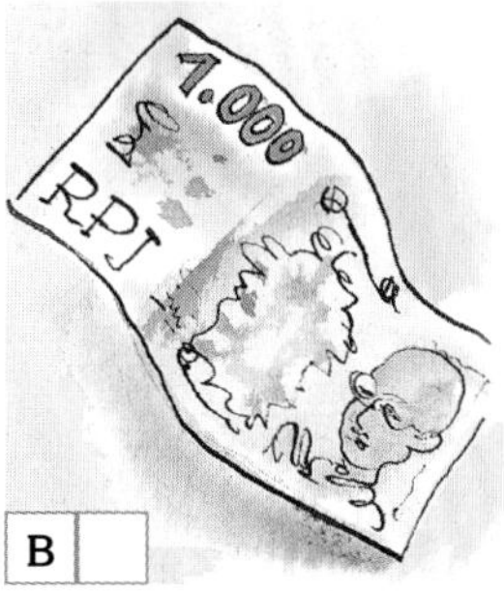

3 Where was the platform?

4 How old was the tiger?

A

B

C

5 What did Mrs Packletide shoot?

A

B

C

6 How was the goat?

A

B

C

PART ONE

Mrs Packletide shoots a tiger

Mrs Packletide was in India. She wanted to kill a tiger. She wanted to shoot [1] a tiger for a special reason. Her friend, Loona Bimberton, flew in a plane. Loona talked about the plane all the time. Mrs Packletide was jealous of her friend's adventure. She wanted an adventure as well.

1. **shoot** : kill with a gun.

Mrs Packletide had a plan. She wanted some journalists to take photographs of her with the dead tiger. Then she wanted to invite Loona Bimberton to lunch, and to give her a tiger-claw brooch. [1] She wanted her friend to be jealous!

Mrs Packletide offered the Indians in the village 1,000 rupees [2] for a tiger. The Indians knew about a very old tiger in the area. It was not a dangerous animal. Mrs Packletide was very happy.

The Indians prepared a platform high up in a tree for Mrs Packletide and her companion, [3] Miss Mebbin. The two ladies climbed onto the platform one night. The Indians put a goat [4] on the ground in front of the tree. Tigers like to eat goats. Mrs Packletide and Miss Mebbin waited for the tiger to come.

'Is this really dangerous?' Miss Mebbin asked.

'Not at all!' Mrs Packletide told her. 'The tiger is very old. He can't jump up into the tree. We're safe here.'

'Why are you paying 1,000 rupees then?' Miss Mebbin wanted to know. 'The tiger's old — it's not worth 1,000 rupees.'

Miss Mebbin was always interested in money. She liked to save money. It gave her pleasure to save money.

Suddenly, the tiger moved out of the darkness. It saw the

1. **tiger-claw brooch** : 
2. **rupees** : the money used in India.
3. **companion** : a woman who is paid and accompanies another woman on her travels.
4. **goat** : 

goat on the ground. It came very close, and then it lay down. It seemed[1] tired.

'It looks ill!' Miss Mebbin said very loudly.

'Be quiet!' Mrs Packletide commanded.

The tiger now got up and began to walk towards the goat again.

'Shoot now!' Miss Mebbin suggested. 'Don't let it go near the goat. Then we won't have to pay for the goat. We can save some money.'

Mrs Packletide picked up her rifle.[2] She fired quickly. The noise of the rifle was very loud. The tiger jumped into the air and then fell to the ground. It did not move. The Indians were very excited. They immediately ran forward. They looked at the dead tiger. They were very pleased.

Mrs Packletide was pleased, too. She thought about her friend Loona Bimberton. 'Something is wrong,' Louisa Mebbin said to Mrs Packletide. 'You shot the goat,' she told Mrs Packletide.

She indicated the goat. It was true. The goat had a bullet-wound.[3] There was no bullet-wound on the tiger, but it, too, was dead. The old tiger was dead from a heart attack!

At first Mrs Packletide was angry. Then she thought about it. She still had a dead tiger. The Indians had their 1,000 rupees.

1. **seemed** : looked.
2. **rifle** : a large gun (see the picture on page 59).
3. **bullet-wound** : a hole made by the rifle.

Go back to the text

PET **1** **Look at the statements below about Part One. Decide if each statement is correct or incorrect. If it is correct, write A as your answer. If it is not correct, write B as your answer.**

1 Mrs Packletide was jealous of her friend's adventure.

2 Mrs Packletide's plan was to invite her friend to lunch and give her a tiger-claw brooch.

3 Mrs Packletide offered the Africans in the village 1,000 rupees for the tiger.

4 The tiger was young and dangerous.

5 It was a pleasure for Miss Mebbin to save money.

1 ..... 2 ..... 3 ..... 4 ..... 5 .....

Now correct the incorrect statements.

T: GRADE 4

2 **Topic — Hobbies/Sports**
Talk to the class about a hobby or sport that involves animals (e.g. riding, horse racing, dog racing, etc.). Bring a photo of this hobby or sport to class, and use the questions below to help you.

a. What is your hobby or sport?

b. Where is this hobby or sport usually played or practised?

c. Where was it played or practised in the past?

d. Will people still play or practise it in the future?

Now think of a question to ask the class about their favourite hobby or sport.

3 **Survey – Are you envious?**

Say if you agree with the statements below, then use them to make questions to ask 10 different people in your class. The first two have been done for you.

1. You always notice what other people have got.
   Do you always notice what other people have got?
2. If you make a mistake, you don't admit it.
   Do you admit making mistakes?
3. You are angry if your friend does better than you.
   ....
4. You always say bad things about other people.
   ....
5. You never think about less fortunate people.
   ....
6. You are always suspicious when your boyfriend/girlfriend goes out alone.
   ....
7. You often lie about yourself.
   ....
8. You often lie about other people.
   ....
9. You think you are the best.
   ....

Write your results here.

1. ....
2. ....
3. ....
4. ....
5. ....
6. ....
7. ....
8. ....
9. ....

PART TWO

Triumph and disaster

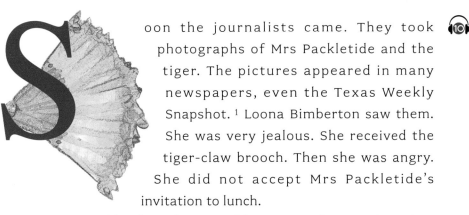

Soon the journalists came. They took photographs of Mrs Packletide and the tiger. The pictures appeared in many newspapers, even the Texas Weekly Snapshot.[1] Loona Bimberton saw them. She was very jealous. She received the tiger-claw brooch. Then she was angry. She did not accept Mrs Packletide's invitation to lunch.

Mrs Packletide and Miss Mebbin returned to London. They brought the tiger-skin with them. Everyone admired it. Mrs Packletide was very pleased and satisfied with her adventure.

1. **snapshot** : photograph.

She went to a fancy-dress party.[1] She wore a Diana[2] costume.

'No one knows the truth,' Miss Mebbin said a few days later.

'What do you mean?' Mrs Packletide asked angrily.

'You didn't shoot the tiger at all,' Miss Mebbin explained. 'You shot the goat. The tiger just died because it was afraid.'

Miss Mebbin laughed.

Mrs Packletide's face went red.

'No one will believe that,' she said quickly.

'Loona Bimberton will believe it,' Miss Mebbin told her quietly.

Mrs Packletide went very white.

'Don't tell anyone!' she said quietly.

'There's a little cottage near Dorking,' Miss Mebbin replied slowly. 'I want to buy it. It costs £680, but I haven't got the money.'

Louisa Mebbin has her little cottage in the country now. It is a very pretty place. All her friends like it very much.

'How does she pay to keep all this?' they all ask.

Mrs Packletide does not hunt tigers any more.

'It's too expensive,' she tells her friends.

1. **fancy-dress party** : a party where the guests wear costumes.
2. **Diana** : from Latin mythology, the goddess of hunting.

Go back to the text

1 **In your opinion, do you think Mrs Packletide succeeded in making her friend, Loona Bimberton envious? Do you think Mrs Packletide is satisfied? Discuss this with a partner.**

2 **In Part Two Miss Packletide has to pay Miss Mebbin because she doesn't want anyone to know that she did NOT shoot the tiger. This is called a bribe. With your partner discuss why bribes are unethical (you can do this in your own language). Then tick (✓) the statements you agree with.**

It is good to pay someone:

a. ☐ for a job.
b. ☐ to pass an exam.
c. ☐ to get a better house.
d. ☐ to cover a crime.
e. ☐ to win a prize.
f. ☐ to cover a lie.

3 **Pretend you are Mrs Packletide and your partner is Miss Mebbin. Complete their conversation and then practise saying it.**

Miss Mebbin: No one knows the truth.

Mrs Packletide: (**a**) .... do you mean?

Miss Mebbin: You didn't (**b**) .... the tiger at all.

Mrs Packletide: No one will (**c**) .... that.

Miss Mebbin: There's a little (**d**) .... near Dorking. I want to buy it . It (**e**) .... £680 , but I haven't (**f**) .... the money.

PET **4** **You will hear an interview with Mrs Packletide about how she shot the tiger.**
For each question, fill in the information in the numbered space.

Mrs Packletide gave her friend a (**1**) .... - .... brooch today.

Her friend is the famous pilot, Mrs Loona Bimberton.

Mrs Packletide spoke about her adventure. There are beastly (**2**) .... in the jungle in India,' she said.

Her companion, Miss Mebbin, was not very (**3**) ....

The jungle is very (**4**) ....

The tiger ran out of the (**5**) .... suddenly.

It ran towards Miss Mebbin.

But Mrs Packletide had enough courage to (**6**) .... the tiger.

5 **The Greek philosopher Aristotle distinguished between things that people want because they are intrinsically good (such as health) and things people want because they can have good effects (such as money).**
Put the words below into each column (you can add more words to the list). Then discuss your choice in your own language with your partner.

sight the existence of diverse species of animals
beauty hearing intelligence luxuries

Intrinsically good	Good because of their effect(s)
Health	Money

Tigers

the world's largest cats

Tigers may look like cats. They have beautiful striped fur [1] and an elegant walk. However, they are certainly not the domestic animals we keep in our homes.

Their teeth can crush you. [2] Man-eating tigers do exist. But the fact remains that humans are more a danger to tigers than tigers are to humans.

Two Bengal tigers swimming.

1. **striped fur** : 
2. **crush you** : (here) kill you by pressing you very hard.

Researchers believe that tigers evolved in southern China more than a million years ago. From there they moved west towards the Caspian Sea, then north to Siberia and south again across Indochina and Indonesia including Bali.

It is very sad that the tigers of Bali, the Caspian region and Java no longer exist.

Of the tigers that live in the wild today, half of them live in India, Nepal and Bangladesh.

There are many projects to help tigers survive in the wild both in India and in Siberia.

Tigers in the snow.

Here are some facts about tigers.

- Tigers need a lot of space. Siberian tigers' territories can be up to 120 square miles (1 mile = 1.6 km.)
- They eat between 20-40 pounds of meat a day (1 pound (lb) = 0.4536 kg.)
- The white spots behind their ears look like eyes to predators
- Female tigers look after the babies, called cubs
- They live in humid, hot jungles as well as icy cold forests
- Their Latin name is *Panthera Tigris*
- They are an endangered species: only about 4,500-7,300 survive today
- Adult tigers live alone
- Tiger cubs weigh about 3 pounds at birth
- Cubs live with their mothers until they are two or three
- The wild tiger lives 10 years on average
- They have excellent vision. They see in colour. At night they can see 6 times more than humans

Mother tiger with cubs.

INTERNET PROJECT

Your teacher will give you a list of web addresses where you can find out more information about these magnificent animals.

Try and find out about:

- why tigers are in danger
- how humans can help tigers survive
- in which cultures tigers are important and why
- why the Chinese use tiger masks for their important celebrations
- which Indian goddess is often depicted riding a tiger
- which schools are involved in 'save the tiger' programmes
- more common facts to add to the list on page 69

Once you have finished your research share your findings with the rest of the class. You can always organise a 'trivial pursuit' type game with the information you have collected.

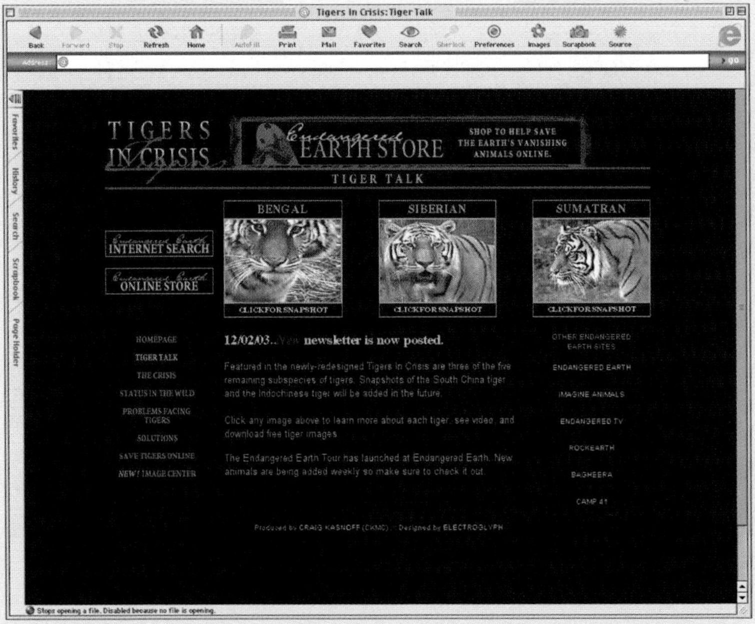

The Stolen White Elephant

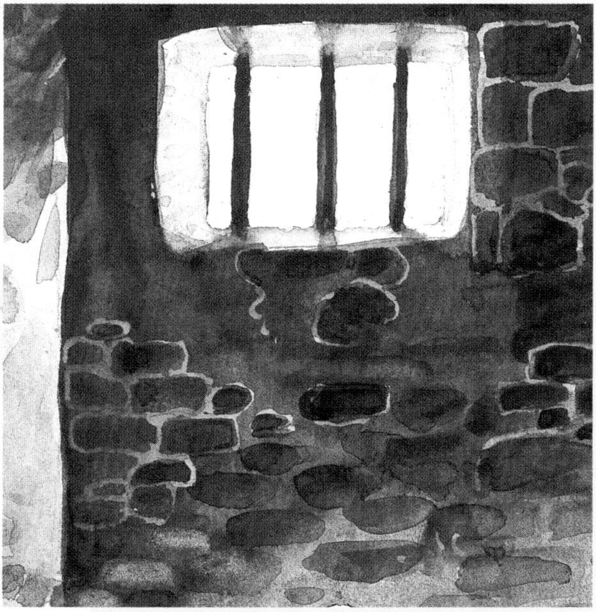

by Mark **Twain**

Before you read

1 **Read the title of the story. 'Stolen' is the past participle of the verb 'to steal' (steal, stole, stolen). It means that someone takes something of yours from you without your permission.**

2 **Now you have the explanation of the title, what do you think will happen in the story?**

3 **Look at the picture on page 75 and describe the elephant.**

a. Where is it?

b. What type of elephant is it?

4 **Did you know that Siam was the name for the country we now call Thailand? 'The Stolen White Elephant' takes place in this country. Find the country on a map and/or describe where it is.**

5 **Use a dictionary to find out the meaning of the words below.**

a. Siamese

b. Siamese cat

c. Siamese twins

PART ONE

A royal present

Once I met a man on a train who told me a story. This is his story.

The white elephant is a very important animal in Siam.[1] Only the king can possess one. Many years ago Britain and Siam argued about the frontier line of Siam. Siam was wrong, and the two countries soon became friends again. The king of Siam decided to send the British queen a magnificent present — a white elephant. It was my job to transport the white elephant from Siam to England. We left Siam in a ship with the elephant, and at last we arrived in New York. We decided to send the elephant to New Jersey for a while. He needed rest after the first part of the long voyage.

1. **Siam** : the old name for Thailand.

Then, a terrible thing suddenly happened — someone stole the white elephant! I went to the New York police.

The chief detective was called Inspector Blunt. He listened to my story in silence.

'This is not an ordinary case,' he said. 'Do not talk to the reporters. I will manage them. Now,' he said, 'what's the elephant's name?'

'Hassan Ben Ali Ben Selim Abdallah Mohammed Moisé Alhammal Jamsetjejeebhoy Dhuleep Sultan Ebu Bhudpoor,' I told him.

'Good. First name?'

'Jumbo.'

'Are his parents living?'

'No, they're dead.'

'Was he the only child?'

'Yes, he was.'

'Now describe it,' Inspector Blunt commanded me. I began describing the white elephant. 'Height, 19 feet; [1] length of trunk, 16 feet; length of tail, 6 feet; total length including trunk and tail, 48 feet; color of the elephant, a dull [2] white; he has the habit of spraying people with water; he has a small scar [3] under his arm.'

The detective wrote everything down.

'Now I want a photograph,' Inspector Blunt told me.

I gave him a photograph of the white elephant.

Then he rang a bell and a boy came in.

1. **feet** : 1 foot = 0.348 metres.
2. **dull** : dirty.
3. **scar** : mark after an injury.

'Make 50,000 copies of this description and photograph, Alaric,' he ordered the boy. 'Give them to all the detective offices.'

Alaric left the room.

'We will have to offer a reward,' [1] Inspector Blunt told me.

'How much?' I asked.

'To begin with, $25,000,' the inspector told me. 'These thieves [2] are very clever and they have friends everywhere — '

'Do you know who they are?' I asked in great surprise and astonishment.

'We usually have an idea who the criminal is,' he told me.

Inspector Blunt then asked me about the food that the elephant ate.

'Men — does he eat men?' the inspector asked.

'Oh, yes,' I replied. 'But he will eat anything. He will eat books, bottles, clothes, cats, potatoes, rice — anything at all!'

'Good, but we need details. Details are necessary. During one day, how many men will he eat, if they are fresh?'

'He does not care if they are fresh or not. At a single meal he can eat five men.'

'What nationalities does he prefer?'

'He doesn't care about nationalities, but he prefers people he knows.'

'What does he drink?' the inspector wanted to know.

'He drinks anything, as well,' I told him.

'These are unusual facts,' the inspector commented. 'They will help us to find the elephant.'

1. **reward** : money for finding the elephant.
2. **thieves** : robbers.

Go back to the text

1 **'The king of Siam decided to send the British queen a magnificent present.' But the present goes to New York and then to New Jersey (USA).**

a. Do you think this is important to the story?

b. Who do you think the British Monarch at the time of the story was?

- Queen Elizabeth I
- Queen Victoria
- Queen Elizabeth II

2 **Look at a map of the United States of America and find the places below.**

a. New York **b.** New Jersey **c.** Pennsylvania

Say where they are: in the north, south, east, west, north west etc. of the USA.

PET **3** **Based on the story and your general knowledge, decide if each statement is correct or incorrect. If it is correct, write A as your answer. If it is not correct, write B as your answer.**

1 Someone stole the white elephant.
2 The chief detective's name was Inspector Sharp.
3 The inspector wanted to know the elephant's name.
4 Elephants eat humans.
5 The reward for finding the elephant was $50,000.
6 The elephant doesn't drink anything.

1 ..... 2 ..... 3 ..... 4 ..... 5 ..... 6 .....

Now correct the incorrect statements.

4 Vocabulary

A voyage is a journey by sea from one place, port or country to another, especially a journey by water or in space to a distant place or country. In the past many discoverers of distant lands went on long voyages. Today, we can read about their exciting voyages in biographies and journals.
Below is a list of famous discoverers (a-e). Match them with the lands they discovered (1-5).

a. ☐ Christopher Columbus (1451- 1506)
b. ☐ Abel Tasman (1603-59)
c. ☐ Vitus Bering (1680-1741)
d. ☐ Pedro Alvares Cabral (*c.* 1467-1520)
e. ☐ Thomas Cook (1728-1779)

1. New Zealand
2. America
3. The Straight of Bering
4. Cook Islands
5. Brazil

It is unusual today to go on long voyages, but people travel today more than they did in the past. Many people go abroad on business trips, school trips, holidays etc. They usually travel by plane, train, coach or car. Ask your partner how he/she likes to travel.

PET 5 **You will hear a police inspector interviewing someone about a missing person.**
For each question, put a tick (✓) in the correct box.

1 The husband's name is
- A ☐ Lanlow.
- B ☐ Landlou.
- C ☐ Landlow.

2 They live at
- A ☐ 105, Fourth Ave, NY.
- B ☐ 115, Third Ave, NY.
- C ☐ 105, Third Ave, NY.

3 What does the husband look like?
- A ☐ He's tall.
- B ☐ He's very short and thin.
- C ☐ He's very short and fat.

4 What has he got on the palm of his hands?
- A ☐ Hair.
- B ☐ Fur.
- C ☐ Air.

5 Where did the husband go?
- A ☐ To the laundry.
- B ☐ To the barber's.
- C ☐ To the butcher's.

6 How many sets of keys were there in total?
- A ☐ One.
- B ☐ Two.
- C ☐ Three.

PART TWO

Inspector Blunt Gives his orders

Inspector Blunt now called Captain Burns. The inspector described the case to him and then he gave his instructions.

'Tell detectives Jones, Davis, Bates and Hackett to follow the elephant. And tell detectives Moses, Dakin, Murphy, Rogers and Bartholomew to follow the thieves.'

'Yes, sir,' the captain said.

'We'll find your elephant,' the inspector told me.

I thanked him. I liked that man, and I liked the way he approached the case.

The next morning the newspapers were full of the story of the stolen elephant. Some of the newspapers gave the opinions of different detectives about the case. Each detective had a different opinion. All the detectives named the criminals, but they all gave different names. The newspaper articles finished with a mention of Inspector Blunt:

'He knows that the criminals are "Brick" Duffy and "Red" McFadden. He knew that they had plans for the crime.'

I was pleased when I read the newspaper article. It was clear that Inspector Blunt was a very clever detective. I hurried to his office to talk to him again.

'You know who the thieves are,' I said. 'Why didn't you arrest them before the crime?'

'We do not prevent crime,' he told me. 'We punish crime. We cannot punish it until it is committed.'

Then I noticed something strange about the reward for $25,000. The reward was only for detectives!

'What about the public?' I asked.

'The detectives will find the elephant,' he explained to me. 'That is why the reward is for them.'

Now the telegraph in the office began to bring in the first messages from the inspector's men.

FLOWER STATION, N.Y., 7.30 a.m.
Found a clue. [1] Think the elephant is going west.
I am following.
DARLEY, detective

'Darley's a good man,' the inspector said.

1. **clue** : indication which helps to solve a crime.

Another telegram arrived.

FLOWER STATION, N.Y., 9 a.m.
Followed the tracks [1] for three miles. [2] A farmer told me they are not elephant tracks. They are holes he made for planting trees. Tell me what to do.
DARLEY, detective.

The inspector sent Darley a telegram.

Arrest the man. He is one of the thieves.
Follow the tracks.
INSPECTOR BLUNT

Next, a telegram arrived from Hawes.

IRONVILLE, N.Y., 9.30 a.m.
The elephant was here this morning. No one knows where he went. He killed a horse.
HAWES, detective.

Inspector Blunt called Captain Burns.

'Send a lot of men to Ironville,' he ordered.

More messages arrived from all over New Jersey and Pennsylvania.

Then a very strange one arrived. It was from the famous circus, Barnum's. It offered $4,000 a year to use the elephant for advertising the circus. The idea was to attach advertisements to the elephant's body.

'Ridiculous!' I cried.

'Of course it is,' Inspector Blunt agreed. 'Mr Barnum does not know me — but I know him!'

1. **tracks** : marks in the ground left by an animal.
2. **miles** : 1 mile = 1.6 km.

The inspector sent a message to Mr Barnum.

> $7,000 or nothing.
>
> INSPECTOR BLUNT

Back came an immediate reply.

> Agreed.
>
> P. T. BARNUM

A little while later other telegrams arrived.

> GLOVER'S, 11.15 a.m.
>
> Just arrived. The village is deserted except for the sick and the old. During a village meeting the elephant put his trunk in a window and washed the meeting room with water. Some people drank the water and died; others drowned.[1] The whole region lives in terror.
>
> BRANT, detective.

> BOLIVIA, N.Y., 12.50 p.m.
>
> The elephant arrived here and disturbed a funeral procession. It killed two people. Several citizens tried to shoot it. Some of the bullets[2] hit it. Detective Burke and I followed the animal into the woods. The elephant stopped to rest, and Burke came very close to it. He shouted out, 'The reward is mine!' The elephant turned round and killed him with its trunk. I ran away. The elephant chased me back to the funeral procession. The elephant killed more people. I do not know where it is now.
>
> MULROONEY, detective.

That was the final telegram that we received.

1. **drowned** : died underwater.
2. **bullets** : 

Go back to the text

1 Tick (✓) the true statements and correct the ones that are false.

a. ☐ Inspector Blunt knew the names of the criminals.
b. ☐ Inspector Blunt wanted to punish the criminals.
c. ☐ The reward was only for the public.
d. ☐ A telegraph is like a fax machine.
e. ☐ Darley followed the tracks for three kilometres.
f. ☐ Lots of messages arrived from New Jersey and Pennsylvania.
g. ☐ The elephant washed the meeting room with water and the people drowned.
h. ☐ The elephant killed detective Burke with its tusks.

PET **2 Your school newspaper asked you to write a brief article on crime prevention and crime punishment.**

Write your article. In your article you should:

- list major and minor crimes
- list five ways of preventing crime
- list five ways of punishing crimes

Write about 35-45 words.

....

....

....

....

....

....

....

PART THREE

The end of the case

I was very unhappy. The elephant was responsible for many deaths — and I was responsible for the elephant!

There were more telegrams that day from all over America about the elephant. But it was clear that no one knew where it was.

It was the same thing the next day.

The newspapers were tired with the story now. There was nothing exciting to report.

The inspector suggested increasing the reward from $25,000 to $50,000.

Four days passed. There was still no news of the elephant.

I followed the inspector's advice again, and increased the reward from $50,000 to $75,000.

The newspapers now began to attack the detectives. They made rude [1] comments about them.

Only one man remained calm, and that was Inspector Blunt. I admired him very much.

About three weeks after the elephant disappeared, Inspector Blunt had a brilliant idea. He decided to contact the thieves and make an agreement with them.

'$100,000 will be enough,' he said.

'We can't give the thieves $100,000,' I said. 'The detectives won't get anything.'

'Yes they will,' Inspector Blunt told me. 'When there is an agreement, the detectives get half of the money.'

Inspector Blunt wrote two letters, one to the wife of 'Brick' Duffy and the other to the wife of 'Red' McFadden:

> DEAR MADAM – Your husband can make a lot of money if he comes to see me.
> INSPECTOR BLUNT

1. **rude** : offensive, not polite.

He soon received these replies to the letters.

YOU OLD FOOL – 'Brick' Duffy died two years ago.
CHIEF – They hanged [1] 'Red' McFadden 18 months ago.

Inspector Blunt then had another idea. He wrote a mysterious advertisement in the morning papers.

A.-xwblv.242 N.Tjnd – fz328wmlg.
Ozpo, - ; 2 m! ogw. Mum.

He told me this advertisement invited the thief to meet him at midnight the following night.

I arrived at the inspector's office at 11 p.m. the following night with the $100,000. He took the money and he left the office. I waited there. At last he came back. He looked very happy.

'We've made a deal. [2] Follow me!'

I followed the detective down into the basement [3] where the detectives worked. It was dark there. The inspector fell over a large object. Then he cried out excitedly:

'The elephant. I've found it!'

1. **hanged** : 

2. **deal** : agreement.

3. **basement** : floor below ground level.

All the detectives were very happy now. Everybody congratulated the inspector on his discovery.

'Give that man a clue, and he'll find anything!' they said happily.

Then they divided the $100,000, and that was a happy occasion, too.

The next day the newspapers were full of praise, [1] except for one. It said: 'What a great detective! He may be a little slow to find a little thing like a lost elephant. He hunted [2] him all day and slept with his dead body all night for three weeks. However, he found him at last, because the man who lost him showed him the place.'

Poor Hassan was dead. The bullets wounded him fatally. He reached the detective's building, and there, surrounded by his enemies, he suffered and died of hunger.

This adventure cost me $100,000, plus my detective expenses of $42,000. I never worked for the government again. I do not have any money and I am a ruined man. But I admire Inspector Blunt as the greatest detective in the world!

1. **praise** : compliments and kind words.
2. **hunted** : looked for.

Go back to the text

PET **1** **Read the text below and choose the correct word for each space, A, B, C or D. There is an example at the beginning (0).**

The person (**0**) ..A....... the story was (**1**) .... for the elephant, and the elephant was responsible (**2**) .... many deaths. He admired Inspector Blunt (**3**) .... much, so when the Inspector wanted to pay (**4**) .... $100,000 reward he agreed. It was a deal for the detectives to receive half of the reward.
The inspector wrote letters to the criminals, but one of the criminals (**5**) .... dead. The inspector wrote a mysterious message in the newspaper. He offered the thief the reward.
When the person telling the story arrived with the money, the inspector (**6**) .... him to the basement. It was very dark. The inspector fell over a large object. It was the elephant.
What happened? Simple. When they discovered the elephant was missing (**7**) .... fired at the elephant. The shots hit the elephant. There was (**8**) .... fog outside and the elephant was badly hurt. It went to the basement and lay there hungry and injured until it died three weeks later.
The adventure (**9**) .... the government official $142,000. He (**10**) .... admires Inspector Blunt, but he no longer works for the government.

0	**A** telling	**B** saying	**C** writing	**D** speaking
1	**A** responsible	**B** obliged	**C** boss	**D** manager
2	**A** of	**B** on	**C** for	**D** at
3	**A** many	**B** little	**C** not	**D** very
4	**A** the	**B** a	**C** some	**D** an
5	**A** is	**B** are	**C** was	**D** were
6	**A** brought	**B** took	**C** collected	**D** went
7	**A** they	**B** he	**C** we	**D** she
8	**A** thin	**B** much	**C** light	**D** thick
9	**A** cost	**B** costed	**C** costing	**D** costs
10	**A** always	**B** sometimes	**C** still	**D** never

2 **Use a dictionary to find the meaning of these words: a needle, a haystack.**
Now, match the idiom below to its correct meaning.

'To find a needle in a haystack'

a. to find something in an obvious place

b. to find something in a difficult place

c. to find a small object in an impossible place

Do you have a similar expression in your own language?
What is it?

....

'Make' and 'do'

When do we use ***to make*** and when do we use ***to do*** in English?

Look at this example:

*Inspector Blunt decided to contact the thieves and **make an agreement** with them.*

3 **Look at the expressions below for 1 minute. Then cover the page and write down as many as you can remember. Be careful not to make a mistake!**

- make your bed
- make a cake
- make a plan
- make a telephone call
- make a mistake
- do the housework
- do the cooking
- do some work
- do the shopping
- do well

16 **4 Number dictation**

Listen to the conversation and fill in the blands with the correct numbers.

Man: Hello is that (**a**) .... ?

Police officer: Yes, it is. How can I help you, sir?

Man: I'm calling to claim the (**b**) .... reward.

Police officer: The (**c**) .... reward is for the missing guinea pig. Where did you find it?

Man: No, I'm claiming the (**d**) .... reward for the missing needle in the haystack.

Police officer: Sir, I have good news. The missing needle in the haystack reward is now worth $100,000.

Man: What do you mean good news? Do you mean to say it has gone down to (**e**) .... ?

Police officer: No, No, sir it is gone up to (**f**) ....
(**g**) .... dollars.

Man: Really. Tell me what do I have to do.

Police officer: Well, all you have to do is tell me where you found the needle, sir, and the money is yours.

Man: Why, that's easy. I found it in a haystack, of course.

Police officer: How about that!

5 Discussion

With a partner discuss the following questions, then write a short paragraph saying what you think.

a. How does the author show that the police is not efficient?

b. How does the author ridicule the police?

6 Use a dictionary to find the meaning of the word 'blunt'. What is the opposite? Now use these words to write some sentences of your own.

....

....

....

....

....

7 **Here is another detective story for you to read.**
Do you know who Sherlock Holmes is?

> Sherlock Holmes and Dr Watson went on a camping trip. As they lay down for the night, Holmes said: 'Watson, look up into the sky and tell me what you see.'
>
> Watson said: 'I see millions and millions of stars.'
>
> 'And what does that tell you?'
>
> 'Astronomically,' Watson replied, 'it tells me that there are millions of galaxies and potentially billions of planets. Theologically, it tells me that God is great and that we are small and insignificant. Meteorologically, it tells me that we will have a beautiful day tomorrow. What does it tell you, Holmes?'
>
> 'Someone stole our tent.'

Can you think of any other famous detectives?
Do you like reading detective stories in your own language?

The Shameful Behaviour of a Fox Terrier

from *Three Men in a Boat*
by Jerome K. **Jerome**

Before you read

1 Match the names of the dogs to the pictures.

a. fox terrier
b. collie
c. Yorkshire terrier
d. bulldog
e. St Bernard
f. poodle

1 ☐

2 ☐

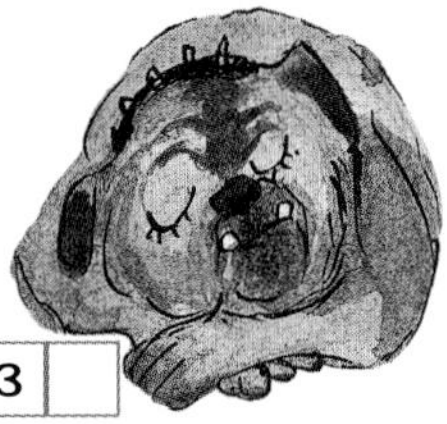
3 ☐

4 ☐

5 ☐

6 ☐

2 Do you know any other species of dogs? Use a dictionary to list what they are in English, and describe them to your partner. Use adjectives like: big, small, ferocious, savage, docile, furry, friendly etc.

3 The title of the story is 'The Shameful Behaviour of a Fox Terrier'. Do you think different species of dogs behave differently? Are there any species you prefer? Talk about your opinions with your partner.

PART ONE

The Haymarket Stores

Fox terriers are about four times more mischievous [1] than other dogs. Their behaviour is shameful. [2] It takes years and years of patience to train them.

I remember what happened in the lobby [3] of the Haymarket Stores. I was in the lobby and there were many dogs all around me. Their owners were inside the shop, doing their shopping. There was a bulldog, two collies, a St Bernard, some Yorkshire terriers, a hound

1. **mischievous** : badly behaved.
2. **shameful** : wrong and ridiculous.
3. **lobby** : large open entrance area inside a building.

E.C.

and a French poodle. There were also a few other smaller dogs. They were about as big as rats.

They all sat in the lobby patiently and silently.

Then a lovely young lady entered the lobby. She had a sweet little fox terrier. She left him there between the bulldog and the poodle. At first he sat and looked around. Then he looked up and started looking at the other dogs who were silent and dignified.

First, he looked at the bulldog who was asleep on his right. After he looked at the poodle who was on his left.

Then suddenly the little fox terrier bit [1] the poodle's front leg. There was a cry of agony in the lobby.

The fox terrier was evidently satisfied with the result of his experiment. So he decided to continue and create some excitement.

He jumped over the poodle and attacked the collie. The collie woke up and immediately started fighting with the poodle. Then the fox terrier returned to his place. He bit the ear of the bulldog and tried to throw him across the lobby. The bulldog attacked everything he could find, including the porter. [2] This gave the dear little fox terrier the opportunity to fight with a brave little Yorkshire terrier.

Anyone who understands dogs will know that by this time there was a great big fight in the lobby with all the dogs. The

1. **bit** : (past of 'to bite') cut with the teeth.

2. **porter** : 

big dogs fought the big dogs. And the little dogs fought the little dogs. At times the little dogs bit the legs of the big dogs.

The lobby was in chaos and the noise was terrible. Soon there was a crowd of people outside the Haymarket Stores. They asked, 'Is there a religious meeting inside?' and, 'Is someone killing someone else? Why?'

Some men came with poles [1] and tried to separate the fighting dogs. Then someone called the police.

During the fighting the lovely young lady returned. She picked up her sweet little dog, who looked at her innocently, and she kissed him.

'My poor little dear, what did those big, bad dogs do to you?'

The little fox terrier looked at her and seemed to say, 'Oh, thank you for saving me from this horrible fight.'

The young lady said, 'The Haymarket Stores must not permit big, savage dogs to stay with gentle, little dogs. This is terrible! I must talk to someone about this!'

And this is the nature of fox terriers.

1. **poles** : long thin pieces of wood or metal.

Go back to the text

1 **Do you think the owner of the fox terrier really believed that her dog was innocent? Discuss with your partner.**

2 **Match the word to the correct definition.**

1. Mischievous
   - A ☐ naughty – non malicious behaviour
   - B ☐ cruel, terrible behaviour
   - C ☐ violent and aggressive behaviour
2. To train
   - A ☐ to put on a train
   - B ☐ to teach an animal or a person to do a particular activity
   - C ☐ to teach animals to bite
3. Lobby
   - A ☐ the front room of a house
   - B ☐ the living room
   - C ☐ the entrance-hall usually to a hotel and/or department store
4. To create excitement
   - A ☐ to have a party
   - B ☐ to make everyone active and enthusiastic
   - C ☐ to make people angry

Now use the above words to write a brief summary of what happened in Part One.

3 **For most native English speakers the following animals have a dominant characteristic. Match the animals to their characteristic. Then discuss your choice with your partner.**

1.	☐ lion	a.	quiet
2.	☐ mouse	b.	proud
3.	☐ snail	c.	clever
4.	☐ fox	d.	friendly
5.	☐ dog	e.	slow

PART TWO

Montmorency

Now the only thing my fox terrier, Montmorency and I don't agree on is cats. I like cats and Montmorency doesn't. When I meet a cat I stop and say hello. I touch it gently. The cat is happy and I am too. When Montmorency meets a cat the whole street knows about it. A lot of bad words fly through the air. Now I know that my fox terrier is not really bad, it is only his nature. But something really unforgettable happened when we were in Marlow.

We went swimming before breakfast and on the way back Montmorency met a cat. As soon as he saw the cat he barked[1]

1. **barked** : made the typical sound of a dog.

with happiness. The cat walked slowly across the street. Montmorency ran after the cat. But the cat didn't run. He didn't understand that his life was in danger.

This cat was big and black. It had half a tail, half a nose and only one ear. It was a clever street cat. Montmorency is a courageous dog but the cold eyes of that cat terrified him.

The cat stopped in the middle of the road and looked at Montmorency with his cold eyes.

The cat and dog did not speak, but their conversation was probably like this:

Cat: Yes! You want me? Can I do anything for you?

Montmorency: No, no thanks.

Cat: If you really want something please tell me.

Montmorency: (*walking backwards slowly*) No, thanks. Nothing at all. Very kind of you. I—I am afraid I made a mistake. I thought I knew you. Sorry I disturbed you.

Cat: Not at all – quite a pleasure. Sure you don't want anything now?

Montmorency: No, nothing at all. Very kind of you. Good morning.

Cat: Good morning.

The cat got up and walked away. Montmorency came back and followed us very quietly. He was silent all day long.

To this day, if you say the word 'cats' to Montmorency, he'll stop walking. Then he'll look up at you as if to say: 'Oh, please don't!'

Go back to the text

1 **Compare the two fox terriers (Part One and Part Two). Write 5 sentences about their behaviour. Look at the table below to help you remember how to make comparisons.**

as ... as	as mischievous as
-er than	bigger than
more than	more aggressive than
less than	less frightened than

a. ....

b. ....

c. ....

d. ....

e. ....

2 **Now go back to page 104. You will hear only the cat's part of the conversation. You must pretend to be Montmorency and act out his part. In order to be convincing you must memorise the fox-terrier's lines. Make sure to sound surprised, frightened, apologetic, etc.**

3 **Discussion**
Discuss the following questions with your partner.

a. Are cats more aggressive than dogs?

b. Are all dogs aggressive?

c. Is it good for people to keep aggressive dogs as pets.

d. Do aggressive dogs need to wear muzzles?

1 Read the summaries of the five stories below. Find the factual mistakes and rewrite the summaries with the corrections.

a. **'The Elephant's Child'**

'The Elephant's Child' is a fable about how elephants obtained their tusks. It is set in the forest in India. The Elephant's Child asks all the people he meets a lot of questions. The baboon helps him and sends him to the small Limpopo River. There he meets an alligator. The alligator pushes his nose until it becomes longer and longer.

Score

b. **'Pigs is Pigs'**

'Pigs is Pigs' is set in Great Britain. It is a story about bureaucracy. Mr Morehouse must pay a sum of money to collect his pigs but Mr Flannery charges Mr Morehouse a lower sum. Mr Morehouse agrees to pay. He writes a letter of complaint to the company. The company is not very bureaucratic and does not reply. Mr Morehouse writes a few more letters. After a short time, the company resolves the problem, there are no more guinea pigs, but the warehouse is empty.

Score

c. **'Mrs Packletide's Tiger'**

Mrs Packletide is poor. She is not very envious of her friend Loona Bimberton. She, too, wants to go on an adventure. She pays some local Africans to kill a young tiger. In the forest, she and her companion hide behind a tree. Suddenly, the tiger arrives, but Mrs Packletide shoots the elephant. The tiger dies of old age and Mrs Packletide can return home with her tiger skin. At last, she can give Loona Bimberton the tiger skin.

Mrs Packletide's companion does not know the truth. She uses it to her disadvantage. Mrs Packletide is happy to give her a cheap house in the country.

Score

d. **'The Stolen White Elephant'**

'The Stolen White Elephant' is a satirical story about robbers. A very small elephant arrives in New Jersey and disappears.

The police must find it. The inspectors look in the most obvious places. They find the elephant very quickly and very efficiently.

Score

e. **'The Shameful Behaviour of a Fox Terrier'**
'The Shameful Behaviour of a Fox Terrier' contains three extracts from *Three Men in a Boat*. The episodes illustrate the good and friendly behaviour of fox terriers. In the first episode the fox terrier does not provoke the other dogs and then pretends to be innocent.

In the second episode, the fox terrier likes to chase rats and make them afraid. But in the end, the rat teaches the fox terrier a lesson. From that day Montmorency adores all rats.

Score

20-24 **2 You will hear a recording of parts of the original stories in this book. Listen and say which extract is from which story.**

1. .... 4. ....
2. .... 5. ....
3. ....

Score

PET **Now decide if each statement is correct or incorrect. If it is correct, put a tick (✓) in the box under A for YES. If it is incorrect, put a tick (✓) in the box under B for NO.**

		A YES	B NO
1	Elephants could not pick up things with their noses.	☐	☐
2	Domestic pets are 30 cents each.	☐	☐
3	Jumbo was born in Siam.	☐	☐
4	Jumbo's parents are dead.	☐	☐
5	The dogs were in the park.	☐	☐
6	Mrs Packletide's intention was to shoot the goat.	☐	☐

Score

Tapescripts

Listing activity, page 66.

Reporter: Good evening. This is Leonard Burner reporting about an extraordinary trophy. The well-to-do Mrs Packletide is very proud about her catch. A real Indian tiger. Today, she met her friend Loona Bimberton, the well-known pilot and gave her a tiger-claw brooch. Mrs Packletide, tell us about your adventure.

Mrs Packletide: Yes, well good-evening to all the lovely listeners out there. What can I say. I went to India in the middle of the jungle, my goodness, with all those beastly animals. You understand, it's thick jungle, where you see nothing but wild animals.

Reporter: Yes, yes very dangerous. Did you go alone?

Mrs Packletide: Well, not exactly. You see Miss Louisa Mebbin, my dear companion would not let me go alone. You must understand that I love Miss Mebbin, but she is not a courageous soul. I told Miss Mebbin that it was dangerous.

Reporter: You mean Miss Packletide that Miss Mebbin did not help you.

Mrs Packletide: Well, I don't want to be rude, but Miss Mebbin is not the ideal hunting companion.

Reporter: Well, Mrs Packletide, please tell the listeners how you managed to kill the tiger.

Mrs Packletide: You see, I had this rifle and well I, we were walking in the jungle, unprotected.

Reporter: Yes...do go on.

Mrs Packletide: And, yes, this big Indian tiger appeared suddenly.

Reporter: How frightening.

Mrs Packletide: Oh, yes. It was awful. It came running out of the thick jungle.

Reporter: My goodness.

Mrs Packletide: It ran straight towards Miss Mebbin.

Reporter: Oh no!

Mrs Packletide: Exactly. I had to save her life.

Reporter: So you shot and saved Miss Mebbin's life.

Mrs Packletide: Well, you know, she is my companion.

Reporter: Yes, I understand. A very brave act Mrs Packletide. A very brave act. Thank goodness you saved her life.

Mrs Packletide: Yes, thank goodness she's alive.

Mrs Packletide: Well, thank you. Yes, thank you.

Reporter: No. Thank *you* Mrs Packletide. And this is the end of...

13 Listening activity, page 79

Inspector: This is a strange case. What is your husband's name?

Woman: His name is Arnold Landlow.

Inspector: Do spell that for me, M'am.

Woman: Yes, Of course. L.A.N.D.L.O.W.

Inspector: Very good. And where does he live?

Woman: Well, he lives with me, of course.

Inspector: The address, the address. I need to know his address please, M'am.

Woman: Yes, we live at 105, Third Avenue, New York.

Inspector: Very good, very good. And what does he look like?

Woman: Oh, inspector, dreadful, he looks just dreadful.

Inspector: Come on M'am. I mean can you describe him, please?

Woman: Well, he's short. Very short. He's thin, very thin. And, well, he doesn't have any hair on his head. He's completely bald. Oh, but he has hair on the palms of his hands.

Inspector: Hair on the palm of his hands! You mean, he's a beast?!!!

Woman: No, sir. Well, sort of. No, No he is a man, you know. He's very *clever*!

Inspector: Hmmm, you say you lost him after you went shopping with him.

Woman: Well, inspector, he lost the keys to the house. We went to the department store and made a new set of keys.

Inspector: Then what happened?

Woman: Well, he had to go to the barber's for a shave.

Inspector: Yes, I see.

Woman: And, well I went home.

Inspector: Did you go back to barber's when he did not come home?

Woman: Well, I left the house almost immediately because I had to visit my sick aunt.

Inspector: Did you return home after that?

Woman: Yes I did. I went home and he wasn't there!

Inspector: So what did you do then?

Woman: I went to the barber's, but he wasn't there.

Inspector: Can I see the keys to your house?

Woman: Of course, here they are.

Inspector: Two sets of keys. Listen here M'am, an officer will go to your house with you immediately. But first I must examine these sets of keys. In your statement you said you only had one set and...

16 **Listening activity, page 93.**

Man: Hello is that 987365?

Police officer: Yes, it is. How can I help you, sir?

Man: I'm calling to claim the $45,000 reward.

Police officer: The $35,000 reward is for the missing guinea pig. Where did you find it?

Man: No, I'm claiming the $45,000 reward for the missing needle in the haystack.

Police officer: Sir, I have good news. The missing needle in the haystack reward is now worth $100,000.

Man: What do you mean good news? Do you mean to say it has gone down to $10,000?

Police officer: No, No, sir, it has gone up to $100,000. 1.0.0.0.0.0. dollars.

Scores for game, page 50.
1. a. 0, b. 2; **2.** a. 1, 2. 0; **3.** a. 3, b. 0; **4.** a. 1, b. 0; **5.** a. 0, b. 2; **6.** a. 3, b. 0; **7.** a. 0, b. 1; **8.** a. 0, b. 2.

Answer for page 52.
Are you thinking of A GREY ELEPHANT IN DENMARK?

KEY TO EXIT TEST

1 **a.** ... elephants obtained their trunks. It is set ... in Africa. ... asks all the animals he meets. The Kolokolo bird ... great Limpopo River... meets a crocodile. The crocodile pulls ... (Score 7)

b. set in the United States of America... a higher sum... Mr Morehouse refuses to pay. The company is very bureaucratic and replies... writes many more letters. After a long time ... there are hundreds of guinea pigs... the warehouse is full. (Score 9)

c. Mrs Packletide is rich. She is very envious ... some local Indians to kill an old tiger ... hide above a tree. Finally, the tiger arrives ... shoots the goat ... dies of a heart attack ... the tiger-claw brooch. Mrs Packletide's companion knows the truth ... to her advantage. Mrs Packletide is not happy to give her an expensive house. (Score 13)

d. ... about the police. A large elephant arrives in New York ... look in the most obscure places. They find the elephant very slowly and very inefficiently. (Score 5)

e. ... two extracts ... the bad and unfriendly behaviour ... the fox terrier provokes the other dogs ... to chase cats ... the cat teaches the fox terrier a lesson ... hates all cats. (Score 8)

2 **1.** A. **2.** B. **3.** A. **4.** A. **5.** B. **6.** B.

Man: Really. Tell me what do I have to do.

Police officer: Well, all you have to do is tell me where you found the needle, sir, and the money is yours.

Man: Why, that's easy. I found it in a haystack, of course.

Police officer: How about that!